Who Was Princess Diana?

by Ellen Labrecque

illustrated by Jerry Hoare

Grosset & Dunlap
An Imprint of Penguin Random House

For Zach and David Peck—EL

GROSSET & DUNLAP
Penguin Young Readers Group
An Imprint of Penguin Random House LLC

Published by Grosset & Dunlap, an imprint of Penguin Random House LLC, 345 Hudson Street, New York, New York 10014. The WHO HQ™ colophon and GROSSET & DUNLAP are trademarks of Penguin Random House LLC.
Printed in the USA.

Library of Congress Cataloging-in-Publication Data is available.

ISBN 9780448488554 (paperback) 10 9 8 7 6 5 4 3 2 1
ISBN 9780451533647 (library binding) 10 9 8 7 6 5 4 3 2 1

Contents

Who Was Princess Diana?

On July 29, 1981, England celebrated a national holiday. Prince Charles, the thirty-two-year-old heir to the British throne, was about to marry Lady Diana Frances Spencer in the "Wedding of the Century." Thousands of people lined the streets of London. Three-quarters of a *billion* watched on television.

As the crowd cheered, twenty-year-old Diana stepped out of a horse-drawn coach, known as the glass carriage, in front of Saint Paul's Cathedral in London. She was wearing a beautiful white dress and a sparkling gold-and-diamond tiara. Her train—the back of her dress—was twenty-five feet long! The future princess walked into the church on the arm of her proud father, Earl John Spencer. Thirty-five hundred guests stood and watched the real-life Cinderella walk down the long aisle on a red carpet. Charles's mother, Elizabeth II, the Queen of England, and his father, Prince Philip, looked on proudly. Standing at the front of the church was Prince Charles. He wore his dark blue naval commander's uniform and his wavy hair was perfectly combed. The handsome prince could have married anybody, and he had chosen Diana.

“I couldn’t take my eyes off him,” Diana later said. “I just absolutely thought I was the luckiest girl in the world.”

The royal wedding was ready to begin. The Archbishop of Canterbury, who presided over the ceremony, described the day as “the stuff of which fairy tales are made.”

Most fairy tales end “happily ever after.” But real life—even the real life of a princess—is often more complicated.

In the years after her marriage, Diana sometimes felt lonely and sad. Her life was not always as happy as the storybook one she had imagined. But on the day of her wedding—when the whole world was watching—Diana was a happy bride. She couldn’t wait to marry her Prince Charming.

CHAPTER 1
A Noble Beginning

Princess Diana was born Diana Frances Spencer on July 1, 1961. The Spencers had been a rich and powerful family for centuries. They were part of the British nobility, or the wealthy ruling class.

Diana had been born in Park House, a beautiful and large home on the Queen's estate at Sandringham, England. In the 1930s, Diana's grandparents were invited to live in the house by King George VI. Park House was then passed on to Diana's mother, when she had a family of her own.

Diana's father, John Spencer, held the title Viscount Althorp (say: VAHY-kount AWL-trupp). He had been an officer in the British Army and had fought for England during World War II.

The Spencer Family Tree

John Spencer,
the first Earl Spencer

Princess Diana's family history can be traced back over five hundred years.

John Spencer was born in 1455. He owned almost twenty thousand sheep and thousands of acres of land, making him one of the richest men in England. In 1519, Henry VIII, King of England, knighted him, making him Sir John Spencer. His knighthood established a connection between the Spencers and the king's family—the British monarchy—that continues today.

Sir John Spencer's wealth and land were also passed on through the generations. The Spencer family tree includes earls, dukes, barons, and admirals. Diana's brother, Charles, the Ninth Earl Spencer, is the godson of Queen Elizabeth II.

Diana's mother was Frances Spencer, Viscountess (say: VAHY-koun-tis) Althorp.

Diana already had two older sisters, Sarah, who was six years old, and Jane, who was four. Because they were such close friends of the royal family, people often said that each of the three Spencer girls might someday marry one of Queen Elizabeth II's three sons: Prince Charles, Prince Andrew, and Prince Edward!

Charles, Andrew, Edward

When Diana was born, the Spencers had been hoping for a son to carry on the family's name and inherit their fortune. In fact, the Spencers had not even picked out a girl's name! They decided on *Diana* a week after their third daughter was born.

As a young child, Diana often played alone. Her two older sisters were away at boarding school. "Their growing up was done out of my sight," Diana later said.

Diana's parents eventually had the son they always wanted. Charles Spencer was born in 1964, when Diana was almost three years old. Charles became Diana's best friend. The youngest Spencer children had fun exploring all of Park House. The huge ten-bedroom mansion had long staircases with

railings the children could slide down.

Diana was an athletic child. She enjoyed riding her bike, swimming in their pool, and climbing trees. She also liked playing with stuffed animals—and kept many on her bed. She loved her real animals, too. Diana had pet hamsters, guinea pigs, and a cat named Marmalade.

Like many wealthy children, Diana and her brother had nannies. Diana, though, longed to be cared for by her mother. She and Charles

tried to get a few of the nannies to quit and even threw their clothes out the window. But they quickly learned that a new nanny could always be hired to replace the old one.

Aside from those few stunts with her brother, Diana was kind to the nannies. She would help them clean the playroom and do other housework. From an early age, Diana's father taught her to "treat everybody as an individual and never throw your weight around." This meant Diana should treat everyone with kindness and never act more important than another person. Diana followed this rule her whole life.

CHAPTER 2
Dreaming of Love

For most of Diana's childhood, her mother and father did not get along. Diana's father was content to spend quiet days on the estate, reading and hunting. Diana's mother was bored by the slow pace of country life. She wanted to travel and have a life filled with adventure. In 1967, when Diana was six, her parents separated. Frances moved to London and John remained at Park House. Her sisters, Sarah and Jane, were still away at boarding school.

In 1969, the Spencers got a divorce. Diana's father had custody of the children. Diana now lived with him during the week and in London with their mother on weekends.

Diana attended Silfield School near Park House. But there were times when she had trouble concentrating. Her parents' divorce had upset Diana very much. Most of the other students had parents who were still married, and Diana didn't like being different. She was only eight years old and wanted her mother and father to stay together.

When Diana was nine, she was sent to Riddlesworth Hall, an all-girls boarding school. She lived in a dormitory and only came home for holidays and occasional weekends. Diana danced and played the piano. She also enjoyed sports and was especially good at diving. But Diana's grades weren't very good.

Instead, she was at her best when she was looking after others. She worked hard at being kind.

In 1973, Diana changed schools to attend West Heath, the small, private boarding school her sisters had attended. She continued to excel at swimming. But what she was really good at was looking after others. Every week, Diana and a friend visited an old woman who lived near the school. They cleaned her house, did errands for her, and spent time talking to her. Along with other West Heath students, Diana also visited a hospital for the mentally and physically handicapped once a week. Many of the patients were in wheelchairs. Some people are unsure how to act around people who are sick, but Diana easily spoke to each one. Her gentle manner made people smile. Even though Diana was a wealthy girl attending a private school, she never considered sick people, or anyone else, less than her equal. Even as a teenager, she was known for her caring nature.

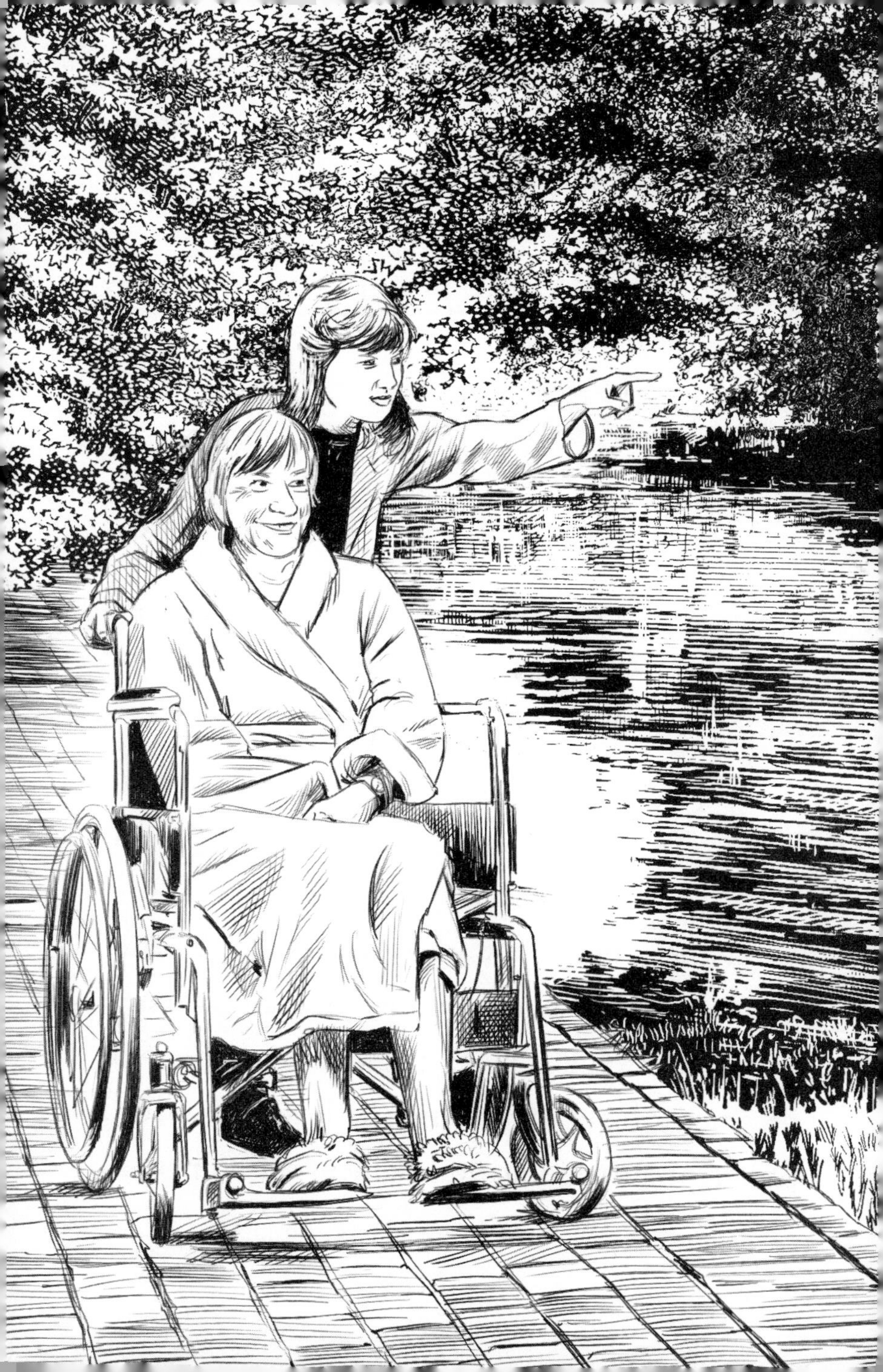

In her free time, Diana loved to read romance novels about young men and women falling in love and living happily ever after. She dreamed of one day falling in love. She had a poster of Prince Charles on her bedroom wall.

Other girls in the school had posters of Prince Charles, too. The dashing prince was a handsome celebrity. He would be the King of England someday! Even though Diana herself was a member of the nobility, she idolized Prince Charles as if he were a movie star.

In 1975, when Diana was almost fourteen, her grandfather, who was the seventh Earl Spencer, died. Diana's father became the eighth Earl Spencer. He and the children moved to Althorp, the family's enormous mansion and estate in Northamptonshire, England.

After her grandfather's death, Diana and her sisters each inherited the title of *lady*. Her brother, Charles, age eleven, became the new Viscount Althorp, the ninth Earl Spencer.

Diana was excited to become Lady Diana. She was less happy to leave her childhood home. But young Lady Diana Spencer was now growing into the noble role she was born to live out.

Althorp House

Althorp is a majestic estate seventy-five miles northwest of London, England.

The estate is on fourteen thousand acres—about the same size as the island of Manhattan. It has ninety rooms, including thirty-one bedrooms. Althorp is filled with rare books, paintings, and furniture that have been collected by the Spencer

family for over five hundred years. Nineteen generations of Spencers have lived on the estate since 1508, when Sir John Spencer purchased it. The property is always passed on through the family to the oldest living male heir.

Today, Princess Diana's brother, Charles, is the owner of Althorp. Parts of the house are open to the public and people are allowed to visit, stay overnight, and even host weddings there.

CHAPTER 3
School and Beyond

In the spring of 1977, when Diana was fifteen, she finished her last semester of boarding school, which was similar to graduating from high school. She still had to take her final exams in math, science, and history.

If she did well on the tests, Diana could go on to college. Even though Diana had been given an award for her volunteer work while at school, she failed her exams twice. But Diana was not upset. She felt that college was not the right place for her. She had even joked with her brother about how poorly she sometimes did at school. But Diana was just being humble. She was smart in many other ways, even if she didn't have the best grades.

Instead of continuing on to college, Diana went to a finishing school in Switzerland.

Diana didn't enjoy finishing school. She didn't like to cook or make dresses. And she was expected to speak French all the time! After only a few months, Diana begged her father and mother to let her come home. Finally, they both agreed. Diana left her school in Switzerland and moved back to England.

Finishing Schools

Finishing Schools, also called charm schools in the United States, taught wealthy young women how to be proper ladies. What did this include? The students learned how to cook, sew, set a table, and host an elegant party. The real goal of the finishing school was to prepare young women to marry rich and important men.

Their formal education was now "finished," and they were then expected to learn the correct manners and social skills to become upper-class wives.

But many women didn't *just* want to marry wealthy men; they wanted the same opportunities as them. Today, many finishing schools have converted into top academic boarding schools.

When she was eighteen, she moved into an apartment with friends in one of the nicest neighborhoods in London. Because her family was so wealthy, Diana didn't need to work. But she wanted to keep busy. She took a job as an assistant kindergarten teacher at a private school. Although Diana had never taught before, her kind and caring nature made her the perfect teacher. She loved working with children.

"She was quite happy to sit on the floor, have children climbing all over her, sit on low chairs beside them, and actually talk to them," the owner of the school later said about Diana.

While working as a teacher, Diana also worked part-time as a nanny for an American family who lived in London. At first, the family didn't even know she was part of the British nobility. They just knew Diana did a great job taking care of their one-year-old baby boy.

Diana spent her nights and weekends going to parties with friends. She attended social and charity balls. Her oldest sister, Jane, was now married to Robert Fellowes, the queen's assistant private secretary. This meant that the Spencers were even closer to the royal family than before.

The parties Diana attended were given by some of the wealthiest and most influential people in the country. On weekends, she traveled back to Althorp to visit her father, who had remarried. Diana's mother still lived in London. Diana, always a pretty girl, was turning into a beautiful young woman. People felt comfortable around Diana because of her kind and easy-going manner. "She could just sit down and make you laugh," one friend said.

Diana was young, carefree, and surrounded by people she admired greatly. She was enjoying one of the happiest times in her life.

CHAPTER 4
Charles

In July 1980, when Diana was nineteen, she was invited to spend a weekend at a friend's home in the country. During the weekend, Diana and her friends went to see Prince Charles play polo at a nearby park.

Polo

Polo is most likely the oldest known team sport. It is played all over the world, but it is the most popular in Great Britain.

Polo is played on horseback, four against four.

Each player uses a long mallet to try to drive a ball across a three-hundred-yard field into the opponent's goal. The winning team is the one that has scored the most goals. Because each polo match lasts around two hours, the horses get tired quickly. Each player rides two to three polo ponies per game.

Prince Charles, whose official title is His Royal Highness Prince Charles Philip Arthur George, Prince of Wales, was the world's most eligible bachelor. Women everywhere wanted to marry him. Photographs and stories about the dashing thirty-one-year-old prince appeared in newspapers, magazines, and on television news shows daily. He was nicknamed "Action Man" because he was athletic and had served in the Royal Navy for five years. It seemed like the prince was always photographed doing something brave—piloting a plane or parachuting out of one. The newspapers also reported details about whom the prince was dating. And he seemed to date a lot of different women. Everybody

wanted to know who the wife of the future king would be.

After the polo match, Diana, Charles, and other friends gathered for a barbecue. While sitting together on a bale of hay, Charles and Diana began talking. Diana told Charles how sorry she was about his great-uncle, who had recently died. Charles had been very close to his great-uncle. He was touched that Diana was concerned about his feelings. The two talked

late into the evening, and Charles asked Diana to go on a date the following week. Then more dates followed. He invited her to a party on the royal yacht, *Britannia,* and soon after, he invited her to visit one of the royal castles for a weekend.

Diana stayed with her sister and brother-in-law, Jane and Robert, who had a cottage on the Balmoral Castle grounds. During the weekend, Charles called Diana many times.

"Charles used to ring me up [call on the phone] and say, 'Would you like to come for a walk, come for a barbecue?' So I said, 'Yes, please.' I thought all this was wonderful," Diana said later.

The Royal Residences

Buckingham Palace

The British royal family calls many different places "home."

There are four crown estates and four private royal residences. The crown estates are owned by the British government. They are Buckingham Palace in London; Windsor Castle in the British countryside; Palace of Holyroodhouse in Edinburgh, Scotland; and Hillsborough Castle in Northern Ireland.

Buckingham Palace is the most famous of these residences. It has been the royal family's London home since 1837. More than 15 million tourists a year visit the grounds of Buckingham Palace.

The four private royal residences, which are owned by the queen, are Sandringham House in Norfolk, England, where the royal family stays during the Christmas season; and Balmoral Castle, Craigowan Lodge, and Delnadamph Lodge all located in Aberdeenshire, Scotland, where the royal family stays during the summer months.

Balmoral Castle

News reporters, who followed Charles's every move, soon noticed Diana. Because she was dating Charles, Diana became front-page news, too. In early September, the British newspaper *The Sun* ran this headline in all capital letters above a story about Charles:

"IN LOVE AGAIN. LADY DI IS THE NEW GIRL FOR CHARLES."

Seemingly overnight, Diana became world famous. If the prince had chosen to date her, everyone thought that Diana must be very special. People wanted to know all about this beautiful kindergarten teacher. When Diana returned to London, photographers took pictures of her everywhere she went. She couldn't get away from them.

"The press were being unbearable, following my every move," said Diana. "They had binoculars on me the whole time."

Even with all the unwanted attention, Diana was falling in love. She was the girlfriend of the future king of Great Britain—the same man she had once hung a poster of on her wall. After dating for over six months, Diana hoped Charles would propose to her.

On February 6, 1981, Charles invited Diana for a candlelit dinner at Windsor Castle, one of the royal homes. Charles, who had been away on a skiing vacation, told Diana how much he had missed her. Then he asked her to marry him. Diana accepted gleefully by answering, "Yes, please!"

CHAPTER 5
The Wedding

Diana and Charles announced their future wedding plans to the world on February 24 in the garden of Buckingham Palace, the six-hundred-room London home of the royal family. Both Charles and Diana seemed nervous as reporters asked them questions about their engagement.

Diana showed off her ring, a sapphire stone surrounded with diamonds. One reporter asked the couple if they were in love, and Diana answered with a shy smile, "Of course." Charles wasn't used to expressing his emotions so publicly. This question seemed to make him feel silly and uncomfortable. Charles responded, "Whatever 'in love' means." Some people thought Charles's answer was odd. They wondered whether the prince was really in love with Diana.

Despite the awkward announcement, Diana moved into her own private rooms in Buckingham Palace two days later. Queen Elizabeth II was thrilled that Diana was going to become her daughter-in-law. She had thought it was time for Prince Charles to marry, and she was happy about his choice of a young, sweet girl from an important family. The queen had even written a letter to a friend describing Diana as "one of us."

With the help of royal officials and the support of the queen, Diana immediately began planning for the wedding. Diana was also busy decorating the country house where she and Charles would live as a married couple. Prince Charles soon left on an official five-week visit to Australia and New Zealand. Without Charles, Diana felt lonely. She also missed the friends she had lived with back in her London apartment.

"I missed my girls so much," Diana said. "I wanted to go back there and sit and giggle like we used to and borrow clothes and chat about silly things!"

Even though planning the wedding had been stressful, Diana was overcome with happiness the night before the big day. She jumped on the bicycle of one of the royal servants and biked around in circles singing, "I'm going to marry the Prince of Wales tomorrow!"

The wedding day, July 29, 1981, was declared

a national holiday in Great Britain. Thousands of people lined the streets of London to see Diana riding in the glass carriage to marry the prince at Saint Paul's Cathedral. Seven hundred fifty million people all over the world watched the wedding on television.

Diana's Wedding Dress

Diana's wedding dress is one of the most famous dresses in the world. Designed by David and Elizabeth Emanuel, it was made from seventy-five feet of ivory silk taffeta and had ten thousand pearls and sequins sewn on it. The dress had a twenty-five foot train—the part of the gown that trails behind the dress. It was the longest train in royal-wedding history. The lace used to trim the dress was nearly five hundred years old! It had belonged to Mary I, the Queen of England in the 1550s. A diamond-studded horseshoe was sewn into the waist of the dress for good luck!

When the wedding began, Diana walked down the long aisle of the church holding her father's arm. When she reached her real-life prince, Charles whispered to Diana, "You look beautiful."

During the ceremony, the bride and groom were nervous. The whole world was watching them! But once the vows were finished, they both smiled broadly and walked back down the aisle arm in arm.

After the ceremony, the newly married couple stood on a balcony of Buckingham Palace and waved to the thousands of people lining the street.

The people below waved British flags and shouted, "I love you." Diana and Charles kissed each other and then went into the palace for a wedding celebration, along with 120 special guests. Twenty-seven different wedding cakes were served, including the official cake that stood five feet high!

The couple spent part of their honeymoon cruising along the coast of North Africa on the royal yacht, *Britannia*. It was hardly a typical honeymoon. The future King and His Royal Highness traveled with a crew of two hundred!

They continued their honeymoon back at Balmoral Castle in Scotland. They had dinner with the queen and her husband, Prince Philip, almost every night.

"There was never any time on our own," Diana said later. "[I] found that very difficult to accept."

The new Princess of Wales, as she would now be known, realized she had much to learn—and many adjustments to make—as a member of the royal family.

CHAPTER 6
The Little Princes

As the wife of the future King of England, Diana was internationally famous. She could no longer go out in public by herself. Crowds of people handed her bouquet after bouquet of flowers. Photographers tried to take pictures of her to sell to magazines and newspapers.

She suddenly had one of the most recognizable faces in the world. The attention overwhelmed Diana. It made her nervous and uncomfortable.

"One minute I was nobody, the next minute I was Princess of Wales . . . It was too much for one person at that time," Diana later said.

Often, Diana kept her head low and her shoulders hunched when she was in public. A newspaper writer called her "Shy Di," and the nickname stuck. The wife of the future king was still only twenty years old.

Charles had been a prince his entire life. He was used to being treated like a celebrity. But, even he was surprised at how popular his wife had become. Yes, Diana was a princess, but she was also an especially *beloved* princess. She had a warm and endearing personality that people adored. When she greeted crowds, she would look people in the eyes, shake their hands, and smile warmly. Once a blind man told Diana he wished he could see her. Without hesitating, she took his hand and placed it against her face so he could feel what she looked like. She hugged children who were in wheelchairs and people who were sick.

Before Diana married Charles, this was not how other royals behaved. The family was reserved—they did things in a calm and formal manner. The royal family kept their distance and politely waved to the crowds that greeted them. Diana was expected to act that way, too. But instead she showed them a much kinder way to greet the public.

At times, Charles joked that although he was the future king, people seemed more fascinated by his new bride. "I know my place now," Charles said. "I'm nothing more than a carrier of flowers for my wife."

In October 1981, Diana learned that she was going to have a baby. She and Charles were both thrilled. Being pregnant made Diana feel very tired much of the time. But she still had to attend official dinners and fancy royal events. She sometimes left early or even fell asleep!

However, seeing the princess appear to be very unlike the rest of the royal family, made people like her even more.

On June 21, 1982, Diana had a baby boy, Prince William Arthur Philip Louis. Prince William is the heir to the heir of the throne.

The Order of Succession

The heir to the throne of Great Britain is the very next person who will become the king or queen. This person is chosen based on a set of rules called the order of succession. These rules became British law in the late 1600s and early 1700s.

Under today's order-of-succession laws, Charles, the Prince of Wales, is next in line to lead the United Kingdom after his mother, Queen Elizabeth II. His son Prince William, the Duke of Cambridge, will become king after Charles. Then William's son, Prince George of Cambridge, will be next.

George's younger sister, Princess Charlotte of Cambridge, is now fourth in line for the throne and could one day become queen.

Charles, Prince of Wales, with his son William and his grandson, George

The queen was thrilled. For the next two months, Charles and Diana were hardly ever seen in public. They spent their time at home caring for their new baby.

From the time William was born, Diana wanted to be a more attentive parent than her mother had been. Diana knew she would have royal nannies and as much help as she needed, but she wanted to be the most important person in her son's life. Diana spent a lot of time with William, hugging him close and giving him kisses. When she and Charles went on official trips, she took the baby with her. This was something new. In the past, royal babies had stayed at home and were cared for by their nannies.

Just a little more than a year after William was born, Diana became pregnant again. Prince Henry Charles Albert David, known as "Harry," was born on September 15, 1984. Like anyone

who married into the royal family, Diana had to adapt to the royal way of life. But she was not willing to compromise the amount of love and affection she showered on her two boys.

CHAPTER 7
Princess with a Purpose

Diana and Charles both loved their sons, but they were having trouble loving each other.

They were very different people. Charles enjoyed reading, fox hunting, and playing polo. Diana didn't share those interests. She enjoyed going to fashion shows, listening to music, and spending time with close friends and family. Sometimes Diana felt lonely, even around Charles and the rest of his family. Diana's grandmother, Ruth, who was the queen's good friend, told Diana, "Darling, you must understand that their sense of humor and their lifestyle are different, and I don't think it will suit you."

Diana was also thirteen years younger than Charles. She wanted to have fun! She wore glamorous designer clothes. She cut her hair short to look more stylish. Journalists took notice and reported on her every move. She couldn't go anywhere in public without being photographed. In an American poll in the mid-1980s, she was voted "the most popular woman in the world."

Diana became friends with celebrities, including singers Michael Jackson and Elton John, and many actors and actresses. When Charles and Diana were invited to the White House by President and Mrs. Reagan in 1985, Diana danced with actor John Travolta.

Photographs and videos of the princess's White House dance became instantly popular around the world. And the dark blue velvet dress she wore that evening became known as the "Travolta Dress."

By this time, Diana had become close with many famous fashion designers, such as Gianni Versace. Gianni loved to create dresses for Diana. He knew that if Diana wore his designs, his name would be recognized everywhere. As with the "Travolta Dress," Diana's clothes and her friends in the world of fashion could become very famous very quickly.

Gianni Versace

Diana had new clothes designed for just about every event she attended.

Her fans and friends gushed over her stunning outfits and how beautiful she looked wearing them. With the help of her designers, Diana became one of the most fascinating and attractive women alive.

While Charles attended to his royal duties, Diana spent as much time as she could with William and Harry. When they went on fun trips to places like amusement parks, Diana and the boys waited in line for the rides just like everybody else. She took her sons out for hamburgers and let them wear casual clothes—like jeans and baseball caps. Diana insisted her boys be raised as close to "normal" as possible. She wanted her sons to experience and understand life, not just as members of the wealthy royal family, but as caring, compassionate people.

As an example to her sons, Diana began to spend more time working for charitable causes. From the time she was a schoolgirl, Diana had enjoyed helping the elderly, the sick, and the poor. She worked very hard at it, too. Diana traveled all over the world—to Germany, Africa, and Japan—to urge people to donate money and time to charities that needed it the most.

When Diana was shown in photographs smiling and spending time with hospital patients and people who were suffering, it made others want to help, too. One magazine article about Diana called her a "Princess with a Purpose." In the 1980s, AIDS was an international health crisis. Many people were afraid to touch AIDS patients—or even be near them because they believed they could catch the disease that way.

AIDS

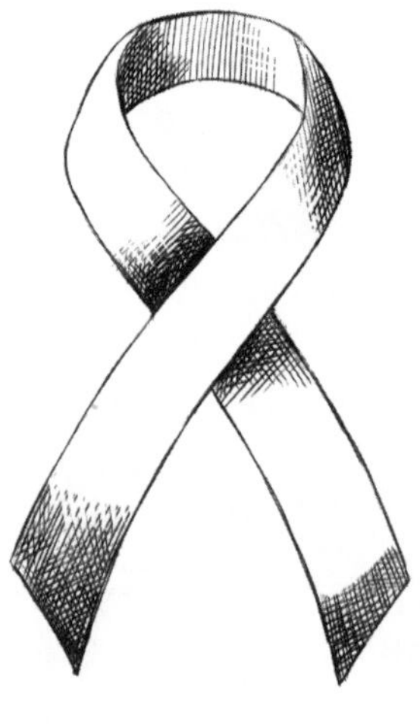

AIDS stands for acquired immunodeficiency syndrome. The cause of this disease is the HIV virus. In the 1980s, it was very common for people with AIDS to die from the disease. Doctors did not understand how to prevent or treat it.

While scientists continue to work to find a cure, there are now medications to help patients with HIV/AIDS treat and manage their symptoms.

In 1987, Diana helped open the first section of a British hospital that was devoted to treating AIDS patients. When she visited the hospital, Diana comforted the patients. At the time, this astonished the public. Diana explained, "you *can* shake their hands and give them a hug—heaven knows they need it."

Diana and Charles were now barely spending any time together. Charles went to business meetings and made official visits around the world. Diana continued to visit patients in hospitals and raise money for the charities that concerned her most. They had only been married for six short years, but when the royal couple was together, they often looked miserable. Newspaper reporters took notice and began spreading all sorts of rumors about Diana and Charles. The fairy-tale marriage seemed to be coming apart.

CHAPTER 8
On Her Own

In February 1992, Diana and Charles traveled together on a visit to India. Charles went about his official business and Diana visited the country's poor. She also had the chance to meet one of her heroes, Mother Teresa, who ran a home for the sick and dying. One by one, Diana visited all fifty of Mother Teresa's patients who were close to death.

Mother Teresa (1910–1997)

Mother Teresa was born Agnes Gonxha Bojaxhiu in what is now the European country of Macedonia. In 1928, she became a Roman Catholic nun and soon after moved to India. She devoted her entire life to helping the poor in Calcutta. Mother Teresa founded a religious order for women called the Missionaries of Charity. She received the Nobel Peace Prize in 1979 for her work with the blind, sick, disabled, and dying. Mother Teresa was declared a saint on September 4, 2016.

"We shall never know all the good that a simple smile can do," she famously said.

Today, the Order of the Missionaries of Charity continues to help people in more than ninety countries around the world.

In March 1992, Diana's father died in London. Both Charles and Diana attended John Spencer's funeral, but reporters noticed that they arrived and left separately. By December, they had officially separated. Diana moved into Kensington Palace in London, while Charles continued to live in their home at Highgrove.

Kensington Palace

When ten-year-old Prince William was told the news about his parents' separation, he responded to his mother, "I hope you will both be happier now."

Both William and Harry lived away at boarding school. When they came home on the weekends, they took turns staying with either their mother or their father. So during the school year, Diana only saw her boys every other weekend. She missed them terribly. Diana remembered how difficult it was for her when her own parents had separated. She tried to show William and Harry more love than ever. "I hug my children to death," Diana said at the time.

Diana was traveling around the world more, visiting homeless shelters and children's hospitals. Because reporters still followed her every move, Diana's visits helped attract attention to places and causes that needed help and money. In November 1994, she attended a reception for the 125th anniversary of the British Red Cross.

By showing her support, she helped raise millions for the organization. In June 1995, Diana visited Moscow, Russia. She presented a children's hospital with new medical equipment and also visited an elementary school.

When it was Diana's turn to have the boys, she often took them on these trips with her. She wanted William and Harry to see the world and grow into caring and kind people, too.

"I want them to have an understanding of people's emotions, of people's insecurities, people's distress, of their hopes and dreams," she explained.

On August 28, 1996, Diana and Charles finally divorced. Although they had been living separately for years, the divorce made everything official. It was very big news.

Nobody wanted the fairy-tale marriage to end. Charles and Diana were supposed to live happily ever after.

The couple agreed to share equal time with their boys. Diana was allowed to keep her home at Kensington Palace, but she would no longer be called Her Royal Highness. Her title remained Princess of Wales.

After the divorce, Diana began to blossom. William's hope for his mother seemed to come true. She did seem happier following her own set of rules. And Diana was as popular as ever. People were especially curious about who she might begin dating after her marriage to Prince Charles had ended. Photographers still hounded her everywhere she went.

"I would come back to my car and find six freelance photographers jumping around me," Diana once explained in an interview.

Magazines and newspapers could sell millions

of copies if they included just one photograph of Diana on a date or in a private moment with a friend. This made life for Diana a daily challenge. She handled the constant pressure with the grace of a princess. She always seemed to smile brightly as cameras flashed and curious reporters surrounded her.

CHAPTER 9
Farewell, Diana

Even though she would have preferred to keep her personal life private, Diana welcomed attention to her favorite causes. She used her celebrity status to help people in need. In late 1996, Diana turned her attention to helping victims who had been injured from hidden explosive land mines. Land mines are small bombs that have been buried in battlefields during wartime to prevent the enemy from advancing. After a war ends, land mines are often forgotten, and they can harm innocent people who step on the unmarked explosives.

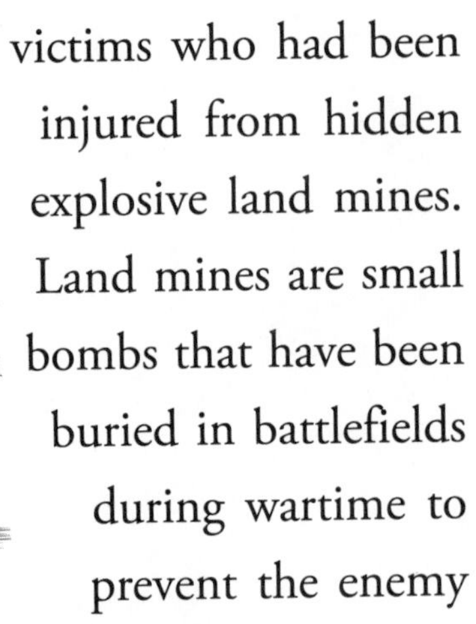

Working with the Red Cross in January 1997, Diana visited the African country of Angola. A civil war had been going on in Angola for twenty years, and fifteen *million* mines—forgotten weapons—were scattered across the country. Close to fifty thousand people—including children—had lost an arm or leg in land-mine accidents. When Diana visited Angola, her goal was to achieve a worldwide ban on land mines.

She wanted to be sure that these small, yet deadly, weapons could never be used again. Just as she had done with AIDS patients years before, Diana talked to and comforted the land-mine victims—many of whom had been injured simply by walking in the countryside. She soon made sure the world cared about this issue, too.

In June 1997, Diana used her own clothing to raise money. At Christie's, an auction house in New York City, seventy-nine of Diana's most beautiful gowns and dresses were each sold to the highest bidder.

The "Travolta Dress" alone was purchased for $222,500. It was the most expensive piece of clothing Christie's had ever sold. In total, the dresses earned $3.25 million. The money was used to help cancer and AIDS patients.

But the world was interested in more than just Diana's charitable work. Less than a year after her divorce, she began dating Dodi Fayed. He was a billionaire whose family owned Harrods, the famous British department store. Some people did not think Dodi was the right choice for Diana. He liked to spend his money on fancy cars, big boats, and expensive

parties. But Diana liked him. She even introduced him to her sons, William, now fifteen, and Harry, age twelve. In the summer of 1997, they took the boys on a vacation to the South of France.

On August 30, Diana and Dodi visited Paris. They went out to dinner at the Ritz Hotel in the heart of the city. After finishing their meal, Diana and Dodi tried to sneak out the back door of the hotel. They wanted to avoid the photographers—called paparazzi—waiting to take pictures of them.

Hotel Ritz, Paris

Paparazzi (say: pa-pu-ROT-see)

Paparazzi is an Italian word that refers to photographers who take pictures of celebrities. While they often try to get their photos in public places, the paparazzi are also known to track famous people while they are simply going about their daily lives: having dinner, relaxing on a vacation, or even shopping for groceries.

Some paparazzi intentionally try to make a famous person angry in order to get a more valuable photo. The paparazzi are often accused of invading the personal space and the privacy of their subjects.

Diana and Dodi hopped into a black car, and their driver sped away. The paparazzi began chasing them in their cars, motorcycles, and scooters, desperate to get a photograph. A picture of the couple could be sold for thousands of dollars. Dodi's driver sped up to try to get away from the cameramen. The driver was going too fast and lost control. The car crashed into a concrete pillar inside a Paris tunnel. Dodi and the driver died instantly in the accident. Diana was taken to the hospital, and she died shortly after. Princess Diana was only thirty-six years old.

CHAPTER 10
Sadness and Grief

The world was devastated by Diana's death. In her honor, mourners left twenty million pounds—ten thousand *tons*!—of flowers in front of Buckingham Palace. Diana's family and friends blamed her death on the photographers who had been following Diana that night. Her brother,

Charles, thought that the magazines and newspapers that bought the photographs were also to blame because they encouraged the paparazzi to be so aggressive.

The royal family mourned quietly and privately over the loss of Diana. On the night before her funeral, the queen spoke lovingly of her former daughter-in-law.

"So what I say to you now, as your queen and as a grandmother, I say from my heart," she began. "[Diana] was an exceptional and gifted human being. In good times and bad, she never lost her capacity to smile and laugh, nor to inspire others with her warmth and kindness."

Diana's funeral was held on September 6, 1997. Her coffin was driven through the streets of London on a horse-drawn carriage. In addition to Diana's family, there were also five hundred more people walking behind her coffin.

These people—who had suffered from illnesses such as AIDS and cancer—were the ones who had been helped the most by the charities Diana supported during her lifetime. The carriage route was made even longer so that all the people who lined the streets could see it pass. More than 2.5 billion people watched the service on television, making it one of the most watched events in history.

Diana's brother, Charles, began his speech at the funeral with these words: "I stand before you today, the representative of a family in grief, in a country in mourning, before a world in shock."

Sir Elton John, Diana's good friend, sang his song "Candle in the Wind" with special lyrics written just for Diana. In one verse he sang,

You called out to our country
And you whispered to those in pain
Now you belong to heaven
And the stars spell out your name

Elton John (1947–)

Elton John is an English singer, songwriter, composer, and pianist. He has sold more than 250 million albums and has written songs for movies and Broadway, including *The Lion King*.

He established the Elton John AIDS Foundation, which has raised over 349 million dollars for the fight against HIV/AIDS.

In 1998, Elton was knighted by Queen Elizabeth II and became Sir Elton Hercules John. His revised song "Candle In the Wind 1997," which was sung at Princess Diana's funeral, is the most successful pop single in history. It has sold more than thirty million copies.

Some of the most famous people in the world attended Diana's funeral, including then First Lady Hillary Clinton, director Steven Spielberg, movie stars Tom Cruise and Tom Hanks, and designer Donatella Versace.

After a private ceremony at her family home, Diana was buried on an island in a lake on the Althorp estate. A path leading up to her gravesite is lined with thirty-six oak trees, one to mark each year of her life.

CHAPTER 11
Her Royal Legacy

Today, Diana's spirit and legacy live on, especially in her children. Her oldest son, William, is married to Catherine Elizabeth "Kate" Middleton, who is called the Duchess of Cambridge. Will and Kate met in college at the University of Saint Andrew's in Scotland.

Kate didn't have a royal—or even noble—childhood, but her kind and gentle personality reminds many people of Diana. William has said that not a day goes by that he doesn't think about his mother.

Prince Harry was in the military for ten years, serving in the Army Air Corps. In 2014, he founded the Invictus Games, an international multi-sport event for wounded veterans. Harry said he realized he had "a responsibility to help all veterans, who had made huge personal sacrifices for their countries."

"I believe I've got a lot of my mother in me," Harry said. Referring to her history of charitable work, he has said, "I want to try to carry it on to make her proud."

Diana's life didn't turn out to have the fairy-tale ending she had once hoped for. But she became the "People's Princess" for all the kind and generous things she accomplished.

Diana had a special way of wanting to help anyone who might need her attention. It made people want to know her, to be around her, and, sometimes, just to see her. She was considered to be as beautiful on the inside as she was on the outside. She became an international celebrity and one of the world's most admired women. In Diana's short life, she made the world a better place. She made people understand that acts of simple kindness are what matter the most.

"I knew what my job was," Diana once said. "It was to go out and meet the people and love them."

Timeline of Princess Diana's Life

1961	Diana Frances Spencer is born July 1 at Park House in Norfolk, England
1969	Parents divorce
1970	Sent to boarding school at Riddlesworth Hall
1975	Diana and her family move to the Althorp estate in Northamptonshire, England
1979	Moves to London and begins working as a teacher and nanny
1981	Marries Charles on July 29 in the "Wedding of the Century"
1982	First son, Prince William, is born on June 21
1984	Second son, Prince Harry, is born on September 15
1987	Visits the first British hospital ward for AIDS patients
1992	Diana and Charles announce their separation on December 9
1996	They officially divorce on August 28
1997	Working with the Red Cross, Diana visits the war-torn country of Angola
	Diana is killed in a car crash on August 31

Timeline of the World

1961	The Peace Corps, a volunteer program that helps people around the world, is founded
1962	John Glenn becomes the first American to orbit the Earth
1963	Civil Rights leader Dr. Martin Luther King Jr. delivers "I Have a Dream" speech
1969	Neil Armstrong becomes the first man to walk on the moon
1979	Margaret Thatcher becomes the first woman Prime Minister of the United Kingdom
1982	The movie *ET* is released
1983	Sally Ride becomes the first American woman in space
1985	The wreckage of the *Titanic* is found on the floor of the Atlantic Ocean
1990	Nelson Mandela is freed from prison
1994	Channel tunnel, or the "Chunnel," opens, connecting the United Kingdom and France
1997	*Harry Potter and the Philosopher's Stone,* the first in the seven-book series, is published in the UK

Bibliography

*** Books for young readers**

Bradford, Sarah. ***Diana: Finally the Complete Story***. New York: Viking, 2006.

Brown, Tina. ***The Diana Chronicles***. New York: Anchor Books, 2007.

Harmon, Melissa Burdick. ***Diana: The People's Princess***. New York: Metro Books, 2002.

King, Larry. ***The People's Princess***. New York: Crown, 2007.

*Mattern, Joanne. ***Princess Diana***. New York: DK Publishing, 2006.

Morton, Andrew. ***Diana: Her True Story***. New York: Pocket Books, 1992.